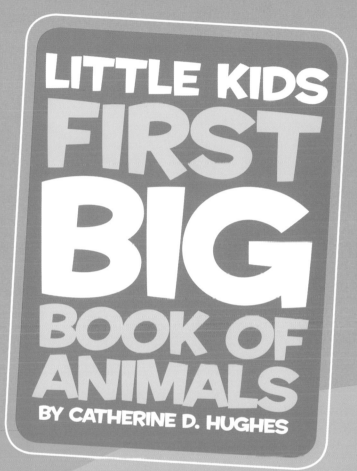

LITTLE KIDS
FIRST
BIG
BOOK OF
ANIMALS

BY CATHERINE D. HUGHES

NATIONAL
GEOGRAPHIC
KiDS

WASHINGTON, D.C.

Published by National Geographic Partners, LLC.

NATIONAL GEOGRAPHIC and Yellow Border Design are trademarks of the National Geographic Society, used under license.

Since 1888, the National Geographic Society has funded more than 14,000 research, conservation, education, and storytelling projects around the world. National Geographic Partners distributes a portion of the funds it receives from your purchase to National Geographic Society to support programs including the conservation of animals and their habitats. To learn more, visit natgeo.com/info.

For more information, visit nationalgeographic.com, call 1-877-873-6846, or write to the following address:

National Geographic Partners, LLC
1145 17th Street N.W.
Washington, DC 20036-4688 U.S.A.

For librarians and teachers: nationalgeographic.com/books/librarians-and-educators

More for kids from National Geographic: natgeokids.com

National Geographic Kids magazine inspires children to explore their world with fun yet educational articles on animals, science, nature, and more. Using fresh storytelling and amazing photography, *Nat Geo Kids* shows kids ages 6 to 14 the fascinating truth about the world—and why they should care. **kids.nationalgeographic.com/subscribe**

For rights or permissions inquiries, please contact National Geographic Books Subsidiary Rights: bookrights@natgeo.com

Library of Congress Cataloging-in-Publication Data
Hughes, Catherine D.
  Little kids first big book of animals / by Catherine D. Hughes.
      p. cm.
  Includes index.
  ISBN 978-1-4263-0704-1 (hardcover : alk. paper) -- ISBN 978-1-4263-0721-8 (lib. bdg. : alk. paper)
  1. Animals--Juvenile literature. I. Title. II. Title: First big book of animals.
  QL49.H8475 2010
  590--dc22
                                            2009050592

Printed in China
23/PPS/19

Acknowledgments
Ray Carthy, Ph.D., Florida Cooperative Unit, University of Florida
Verena Gill, U.S. F.W.S. Marine Mammals Management Office, Sea Otter Program
Eleanor Lee, The Penguin Project, University of Washington
Erica McKenzie, Ph.D., Oregon State University
Alistair Melzer, Ph.D., Koala Research Centre of Central Queensland
Robert K. Robbins, Ph.D., Smithsonian Institution, National Museum of Natural History
Michelle Rodrigues, Ohio State University
David Scheel, Ph.D., Alaska Pacific University
Andrei Sourakov, Florida Museum of Natural History
Mary Ann Teitelbaum, Ph.D., Amherst Exempted Village School District, Ohio
A special thanks to Kimberly, Luke, Emma, and Elise Smith for their invaluable help with this book.

CONTENTS

GRASSLAND

Grasses are the main plants that grow in grasslands. There are not many trees here.

FACTS

KIND OF ANIMAL
mammal

HOME
parts of Africa and Asia

SIZE
about as tall as a large dog

FOOD
gazelles, impalas, hares, and other animals

SOUNDS
chirp, twitter, hiss, purr

BABIES
two to five at a time; usually three

Cheetahs **RUN FASTER** than any other land animal—65 miles an hour. That is as fast as a car drives on a highway.

CHEETAH

Cheetah cubs play games.

A cheetah family wakes up early. The mother cheetah goes to hunt for food.

A cheetah's **LONG TAIL** helps it **BALANCE** when it makes **SHARP TURNS.**

Cheetah cubs climb on a tree. When a cheetah is up high, it can see far away.

9

Cheetah cubs play games. They chase each other and pounce. Sometimes they pounce on top of each other.

"CHEETAH" comes from *chita*, a word in the Hindi language that means "spotted."

Adult cheetahs can run very fast. Baby cheetahs practice running like their mother.

ADULT

BABY

Imagine six **FOUR-YEAR-OLD KIDS** lying in a line, head to feet. That is the **DISTANCE** that a running cheetah covers with **EACH STEP**.

The mother cheetah protects her cubs. She watches them play. When a cub gets tired, Mom is there for snuggle time.

Can you count the number of times the word "cheetah" appears in this story?

ZEBRA

Stripes confuse enemies.

A zebra looks like a horse with stripes. Every zebra's stripes are a little bit different.

Zebras **SLEEP STANDING** up.

Zebras live in family groups called herds. It is important for a zebra family to stay together for protection.

There are **THREE SPECIES,** or kinds, of zebras.

Zebras' stripes confuse animals that hunt them. The jumble of stripes makes it hard to see where one zebra ends and another begins.

FACTS

KIND OF ANIMAL
mammal

HOME
parts of Africa

SIZE
about as tall as a small horse

FOOD
mostly grass, some leaves and twigs

SOUNDS
bray, bark, soft snort

BABIES
one at a time

A baby zebra is called a foal. It can walk when it is only 20 minutes old. An hour after it is born, the foal can run.

How old were you when you learned to walk?

KIND OF ANIMAL
mammal

HOME
parts of Africa

SIZE
about as tall as three men standing on each other's shoulders

FOOD
leaves

SOUNDS
hiss, bellow, whistle, grunt, snort, bleat

BABIES
usually one at a time; sometimes two

GIRAFFE

Giraffes are the tallest land animals.

A giraffe's legs are taller than most grown-up people. Its long neck adds even more to its height.

A giraffe **PROTECTS ITSELF** from enemies by **KICKING.**

Giraffes eat leaves. Because they are so tall, giraffes can reach leaves growing high in trees.

15

Giraffes like acacia leaves. Acacia trees have big thorns. Giraffes can reach around the thorns with their long tongues.

A **GIRAFFE'S TONGUE** is about 18 inches long. It would stretch almost all the way across this open book.

Giraffes do not need much **SLEEP.** You probably sleep about ten hours a night. A giraffe might sleep **ONLY TWO HOURS.**

Reaching a drink is tricky for this tall animal. First the giraffe spreads its front legs.

Then it stretches its neck down to the water. Luckily a giraffe gets much of the water it needs from what it eats.

How tall are you?

BLACK-AND-YELLOW GARDEN SPIDER

A garden spider builds a web.

The garden spider builds a web to trap insects to eat. The web is made of spider silk. Spider silk is a sticky thread that is made inside the spider's body.

BABY SPIDERS are called spiderlings.

FEMALE, or girl, black-and-yellow garden spiders build **BIGGER WEBS** than male, or boy, spiders.

The spider attaches silk threads to grasses or other plants. Then it stretches more silk, making a pattern in a circle.

The spider weaves a zigzag line in the web. That is where the spider usually waits for an insect to fly into the web and get stuck. That insect becomes the spider's supper.

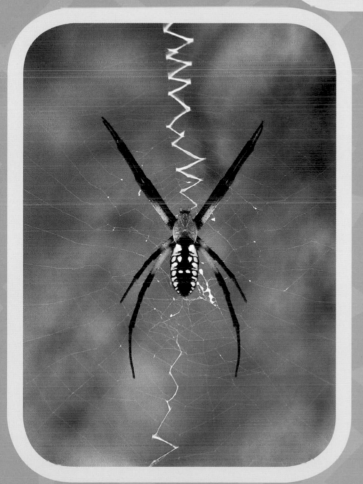

FACTS

KIND OF ANIMAL
arachnid

HOME
much of North America

SIZE
about as big as the spider in the photo at left

FOOD
flies, beetles, wasps, grasshoppers, and other flying insects

SOUNDS
none

BABIES
up to 1,400 eggs at a time

Can you draw a spiderweb?

FACTS

KIND OF ANIMAL
mammal

HOME
parts of Africa and a
small area in India

SIZE
weighs about as much
as one or two men

FOOD
gazelles, zebras, hares,
and other animals

SOUNDS
roar, purr, snarl, hiss

BABIES
three to five at a time

LION

Lions live in prides.

Lions are the only wild cats that live in family groups called prides. Lion cubs have many playmates in their pride.

A playful lion cub finds toys easily. Even a stick becomes a toy.

Cubs chase, leap, and pounce on each other. Playing is great exercise and helps cubs grow strong.

A lion mother carries her cub gently in her mouth. Pet cats carry their babies the same way.

LIONS ROAR to tell other lions where they are.

Which lion on this page has a mane?

A father lion has long hair around his face and neck, called a mane. A mane begins to grow when the lion is about three and a half years old.

23

OCEAN

Most of the Earth's surface is covered by oceans.
Ocean water is salty.

FACTS

KIND OF ANIMAL
mammal

HOME
in oceans worldwide,
wherever waters are
not too cold

SIZE
about as long as three
tricycles in a row

FOOD
fish and squid

SOUNDS
click, whistle, squeal

BABIES
one at a time

There are
more than
**30 DIFFERENT
SPECIES** of
dolphins.

Bottlenose
dolphins may
live to be **20
YEARS OLD**
in the wild.

BOTTLENOSE DOLPHIN

Dolphins must breathe air.

Dolphins live in the ocean. When a dolphin needs to take a breath of air, it swims to the surface.

It breathes through a blowhole on the top of its head the same way you breathe through your nose.

BLOWHOLE

BLOWHOLE

27

A baby dolphin is called a **CALF**. A mother dolphin gives **BIRTH** to a new calf every two or three years.

Dolphins are good swimmers. They use their tails to help them swim through the water.

Bottlenose dolphins can leap high out of the water. Sometimes they leap two or three times in a row.

A dolphin **CALF** can **SWIM** minutes after it is born.

Dolphins are smart. They talk to each other using sounds like clicks, squeals, and whistles.

Can you talk like a dolphin?

GREEN SEA TURTLE

Sea turtles lay eggs on beaches.

Green sea turtles live in the ocean.
Mother sea turtles come ashore to
lay eggs on a sandy beach.

First a mother sea turtle digs a hole.

Then she lays about 100 eggs in the nest. She covers them with sand.

In about 60 days, baby green sea turtles hatch. They are called hatchlings.

The hatchlings all dig out of the nest together. Then they crawl to the ocean. They swim away and grow big and strong like their mother.

Do you like to swim?

There are seven species of sea turtles, including the **GREEN SEA TURTLE** shown in the story. How many sea turtle names can you learn by heart?

FLATBACK

LOGGERHEAD

KEMP'S RIDLEY

HAWKSBILL

OLIVE RIDLEY

LEATHERBACK

SHORT-HEAD SEAHORSE

Seahorses are fish.

A short-head seahorse has a head that looks like a horse's. Its tail looks like a monkey's. It has a pouch like a kangaroo. But it lives in the ocean and swims. The seahorse is a fish.

There are more than **32 SPECIES** of seahorses.

A seahorse can **LOOK UP** with one eye while the other eye **LOOKS DOWN.**

When a seahorse mother lays eggs, she puts them in the seahorse father's pouch. He carries the eggs until they hatch.

FACTS

KIND OF ANIMAL
fish

HOME
waters around south-western Australia

SIZE
about the size of the adult seahorse at left

FOOD
tiny shrimplike creatures

SOUNDS
none known

BABIES
about 50 at a time

Seahorses can **GRASP PLANTS** with their tails. This helps them stay in one place.

Baby seahorses look like their mothers and fathers—just smaller. As soon as they leave dad's pouch, the babies are on their own.

Can you find another animal in the book that has a pouch? HINT: Look on page 84.

SEA OTTER

Thick fur keeps otters warm.

Sea otters are expert swimmers. Their thick, fluffy fur keeps them warm in cold ocean water.

Sea otters make sure their fur is very clean so that it will keep them warm. Otters spend hours every day cleaning themselves.

When a sea otter **DIVES**, its **EARS AND NOSE** close tightly to keep water out.

A sea otter mother floats on her back with her baby resting safely on her tummy.

When the mother dives for food, her baby naps wrapped in seaweed so it won't float away.

A baby sea otter cannot **DIVE** underwater until it is three months old.

Sometimes sea otters **FLOAT TOGETHER** in groups. The groups are called rafts.

Sea otters hold their breath to dive underwater. That is where they find food to eat.

Sea otters like to eat clams and other sea creatures. They use their stomachs as tables when they eat.

Where do you usually eat?

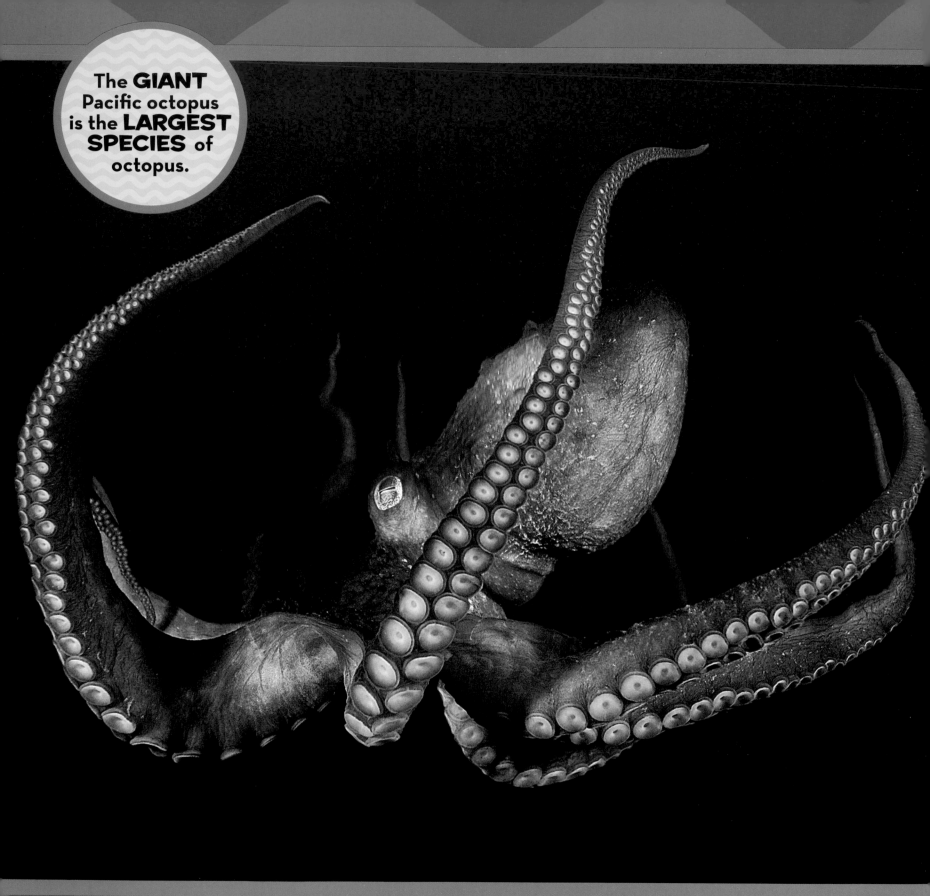

The **GIANT** Pacific octopus is the **LARGEST SPECIES** of octopus.

GIANT PACIFIC OCTOPUS

An octopus has no bones.

FACTS:

KIND OF ANIMAL
mollusk

HOME
much of the Pacific Ocean where waters are not too warm

SIZE
from arm tip to arm tip, about as long as a small car

FOOD
crabs, lobsters, fish, clams, oysters, and more

SOUNDS
none known

BABIES
20,000 to 100,000 eggs at a time

An octopus's whole body is soft and squishy, except for its mouth.

Its mouth is called a beak. It is sharp and hard. The beak is underneath the octopus, in the middle of all of its arms.

ARM

BEAK

41

Can you count the number of arms on this giant Pacific octopus?

SUCTION CUP

The octopus has eight arms. Each arm has two rows of suction cups.

The octopus's two big eyes are on its head. Behind its eyes is a part of its body called a mantle. It looks like a bag.

Octopus **BLOOD** is **BLUE.**

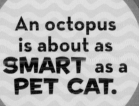

An octopus is about as **SMART** as a **PET CAT.**

Under the eyes is a siphon, which looks like a fat straw. To swim, the octopus sucks water into its mantle and then squirts it out through the siphon. That shoots the octopus through the ocean.

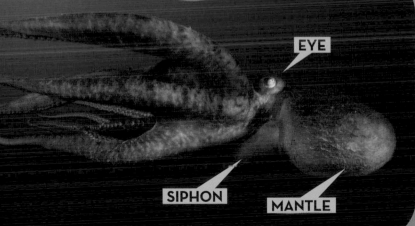

EYE

SIPHON

MANTLE

Male humpback **WHALES SING.** A whale's song can last 15 minutes.

Whales come to the surface of the ocean to **BREATHE.** Humpback whales can hold their breath for up to **30 MINUTES.**

FACTS

KIND OF ANIMAL
mammal

HOME
oceans worldwide

SIZE
about as long as a big bus

FOOD
shrimplike krill, small fish

SOUNDS
squeal, grunt, moan, and sounds too low for humans to hear

BABIES
one at a time

HUMPBACK WHALE

Humpbacks do not have teeth.

There are many kinds of whales. Some have teeth. Others do not.

The humpback whale has baleen instead of teeth. Baleen hangs from the whale's upper jaw.

UPPER JAW

BALEEN

UPPER JAW

LOWER JAW

A humpback whale opens its mouth wide to eat. Its mouth fills with water as well as small fish and other creatures that live in the water.

Then the whale closes its mouth. A curtain of baleen hangs over the opening. The whale uses its tongue to push the water out through the baleen.

Humpback whales often **LEAP OUT** of the water and **FALL BACK IN,** making a big **SPLASH.**

The baleen lets the water out, but keeps the fish and other sea creatures inside. It acts as a strainer. When no water is left, the whale swallows. That's dinner!

Do your parents pour spaghetti through a strainer when it has finished cooking?

BLUE-STRIPED GRUNT

These fish stick together.

Blue-striped grunts move in a large group called a school.

Grunts travel in schools because staying together helps protect them.

Grunts get their name from the **PIGLIKE** noises they make.

FACTS

KIND OF ANIMAL
fish

HOME
western Atlantic Ocean

SIZE
a little longer than this page

FOOD
small fish, other sea creatures

SOUNDS
grunt

BABIES
unknown how many at a time

The school can look like one huge, scary fish to a predator that might want to eat a grunt. It's hard to tell where one fish ends and another begins.

There are many words for groups of animals, such as **FLOCK** of sheep, **HERD** of zebras, and **POD** of whales.

Are there more than ten fish in this school?

All the blue-striped grunts turn, speed up, and slow down at exactly the same time. They don't even bump into each other!

DESERT

Deserts can be hot or cold, but they are all very dry.
Less than ten inches of rain falls in a desert each year.

ARIZONA CORAL SNAKE

Bright colors send a message.

A coral snake's bright colors warn, "I'm poisonous, so stay away!" The colors remind predators, or enemies that might attack, to leave this kind of snake alone.

Arizona coral snakes are small, and their teeth are very short. They use their poison mainly to kill small animals to eat, such as lizards and other snakes.

Arizona coral snakes are **SHY.** They spend a lot of time under rocks or dirt and usually **HUNT AT NIGHT.**

When the snake bites another snake, poison flows through tubes in its fangs—two sharp teeth on its upper jaw— and into its prey.

Have you ever seen a snake?

53

KIND OF ANIMAL
mammal

HOME
parts of southern Africa

SIZE
when seated, a little taller than this book

FOOD
mostly insects, also scorpions, other small animals, eggs, roots, fruits

SOUNDS
peep, twitter, bark, and other noises

BABIES
two to five at a time

MEERKAT

Meerkats have jobs.

Meerkats are almost always busy. They live together in groups. Members of the group work together to help each other.

Meerkats are great diggers. They use their strong claws to dig underground burrows. They dig to find insects to eat, too.

Meerkats take **SUNBATHS.** They stand facing the sun each morning to warm themselves.

Some meerkats in the group act as guards. They warn the others if an enemy, such as an eagle, comes near. The guard calls an alarm so all the meerkats can scurry into their burrow.

A **GROUP** of meerkats is called a **MOB.**

Babysitters take care of baby meerkats while their parents are away finding food.

All the adults in a group help teach the babies how to catch their own food.

When the day is over, the meerkats head inside their burrow to sleep.

Do you have a special job to do at home?

DESERT JERBOA

Desert jerboas hop like kangaroos.

FACTS

KIND OF ANIMAL
mammal

HOME
northern Africa

SIZE
about the size of the
jerboa in the photo at
right

FOOD
roots, grass, seeds,
insects

SOUNDS
rarely make noise

BABIES
two to six at a time;
usually three

Desert jerboas have big hind feet that help them jump. They also have long tails. Their tails help them balance as they hop. Their front legs are short.

By the time a jerboa is **TEN WEEKS OLD,** it is ready to live on its own.

Fur on the bottom of their feet keeps them from sinking into the desert sand.

During the day, desert jerboas stay cool in underground burrows. They come out at night when the sun goes down.

Desert jerboas do not need to **DRINK WATER** every day. They get much of the water they need from their food.

Can you hop like a jerboa?

59

THORNY LIZARD

A spiny body protects this reptile.

Sharp, hard spines cover the thorny lizard's body. Spines help protect the animal from predators.

A thorny lizard can live as long as **20 YEARS** in the wild.

The thorny spines also help the lizard collect water to drink. It does not rain very much in the desert where thorny lizards live.

Early morning dew, or water droplets from the air, collect on the thorny lizard's body.

A thorny lizard eats about **750 ANTS** each day. It picks them up one at a time, using its **STICKY TONGUE.**

The spines help guide the water toward its neck and into the thirsty lizard's mouth.

How do you cool off when you are hot?

CAMEL

Camels have humps.

FACTS

KIND OF ANIMAL
mammal

HOME
Bactrian: dry areas of Mongolia and China; Dromedary: dry areas of North Africa and the Middle East

SIZE
a little taller than a very tall man

FOOD
many different kinds of plants

SOUNDS
moan, groan, bleat, bellow, roar, rumble

BABIES
usually one at a time

You probably know that camels have humps.
Did you know that there are two species of camels?
One has two humps. The other has one hump.

Bactrian camels have two humps.
Dromedary camels have one hump.

Camel humps are filled with fat. The stored fat gives a camel the energy it needs when it can't find any food.

When a **CAMEL WALKS**, it moves both legs on **ONE SIDE** at the same time.

Some people use dromedary camels to help them **CARRY THINGS.**

A camel's thick fur helps it stay cool in the heat of the desert. The fur keeps the sun's heat away from the camel's skin. It acts like a beach umbrella, shading the camel's body.

Can you walk like a camel?

FOREST

Forests have trees. There are many kinds of forests. Some are very dense and wet. Others are more open and dry.

FACTS

KIND OF ANIMAL
amphibian

HOME
parts of southern Mexico to northern South America

SIZE
about as long as the word tree in the title at right

FOOD
crickets, flies, moths, and other small animals

SOUNDS
croak

BABIES
30 to 50 eggs at a time

These **FROGS** hardly ever **LEAVE** the trees.

RED-EYED TREE FROG
Frogs start out as tadpoles.

A red-eyed tree frog mother carefully finds a leaf that hangs over water. She lays her eggs on it.

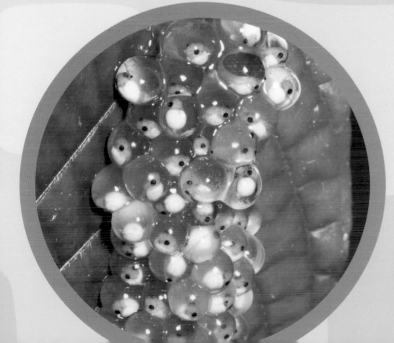

Tiny baby frogs begin to form inside the eggs. The eggs hatch, and the babies fall gently into the water.

69

The babies are called tadpoles. They don't look like frogs yet.

The tadpoles swim, eat, and grow. Soon they grow legs and their tails disappear.

What did you look like when you were a baby?

Red-eyed tree frogs are **NOCTURNAL.** That means they are active only at **NIGHT.**

Now they are adult frogs. They leave the water and use their long legs to jump.

Red-eyed tree frogs have toes like suction cups. Their special feet help them climb. They hunt for meals of insects in trees and on plants.

The red-eyed tree frog's eyes **MAY STARTLE** an enemy, giving the frog a chance to **GET AWAY.**

KIND OF ANIMAL
mammal

HOME
parts of North America,
Europe, and Asia

SIZE
about as big as a
German Shepherd dog

FOOD
mostly large animals,
such as moose, deer,
and bison

SOUNDS
whine, snarl, howl

BABIES
two to six at a time;
usually four

72

GRAY WOLF
Wolves live together in packs.

Young wolves, or pups, grow up in a family group called a pack. Pups have several brothers and sisters.

PET DOGS are closely **RELATED** to wolves.

A baby wolf begs for food by licking an adult wolf's mouth.

73

All of the adults in a wolf pack take care of the pups. They feed and protect the baby wolves.

A wolf can eat about **20 POUNDS** of food at one meal. You'd have to eat **80 HAMBURGERS** for dinner to match a wolf's appetite!

Wolves **HOWL** to stay in touch with each other.

Wolf pups like to play the same games you enjoy. Tag is one of their favorites.

By the time they are six months old, young wolves are ready to hunt with the pack.

Can you howl like a wolf?

BLACK-HANDED SPIDER MONKEY

Monkeys are at home in the trees.

Black-handed spider monkeys are acrobats. They swing from branch to branch. Sometimes they leap to the next tree.

Black-handed spider monkeys rarely come out of the treetops.

When a baby black-handed spider monkey is **ONE YEAR OLD** it can climb by itself.

FACTS

KIND OF ANIMAL
mammal

HOME
Mexico to northern
South America

SIZE
weighs about the same
as a six-month-old baby

FOOD
mostly fruit, leaves; also
nuts, flowers, insects

SOUNDS
whinny, bark

BABIES
usually one at a time

A baby spider monkey clings to its mother's chest until it is about five months old. Then it starts riding piggyback.

If a **BABY** monkey can't reach from one tree to another, its **MOTHER** uses her own body to make a **BRIDGE** for the baby to cross.

Do you like to hang and swing on monkey bars at a playground?

A spider monkey uses its arms, legs, and tail to hold onto branches. The monkey can hang from a branch with its tail. It can even use its tail to pick up a piece of fruit.

This kind of **HANDY TAIL** is called a prehensile tail.

BLUE MORPHO BUTTERFLY

A caterpillar becomes a butterfly.

A mother blue morpho butterfly lays eggs. When the eggs hatch, out come caterpillars!

A blue morpho butterfly lives for about **115 DAYS.**

A caterpillar eats and grows. Then it makes a chrysalis around its body. The chrysalis is a covering that protects the caterpillar inside while it becomes a butterfly.

A brand-new blue morpho butterfly comes out of the chrysalis. It stretches its wings. Soon the pretty blue butterfly flies away.

FACTS

KIND OF ANIMAL
insect

HOME
rain forests of Central and South America

SIZE
about the size of your mother's hand

FOOD
adults drink the juice of rotting fruit

SOUNDS
none

BABIES
unknown how many eggs are laid at a time

Butterflies

There are many kinds of butterflies. Can you count the butterflies shown on these pages?

PROCILLA BEAUTY

AMBER GLASSWING

SCARLET SWALLOWTAIL

DARK BLUE PANSY

ENGLISH COMMA

ZEBRA

KOALA

A koala mother has a pouch.

When a baby koala is born, it crawls into its mother's pouch. The mother koala keeps her baby safe and warm.

A baby koala is called a **JOEY**. When it is born, a joey is about the size of a **JELLY BEAN**.

FACTS

KIND OF ANIMAL
mammal

HOME
parts of Australia

SIZE
about the size of a one-year-old child

FOOD
mostly eucalyptus tree leaves

SOUNDS
wail, bellow, scream

BABIES
usually one at a time

The little koala grows quickly. Soon the furry baby holds onto the fur on its mother's belly or rides on her back.

Koala breath smells like **COUGH DROPS.** The smell comes from the eucalyptus leaves koalas eat.

Koalas spend most of their time in trees. They eat leaves.

Koalas are **MARSUPIALS.** Most marsupials, including koalas, carry their babies in **POUCHES.**

Sometimes a koala must find a tree with more leaves. It walks to another tree.

A baby koala starts to climb trees by itself when it is nine months old.

Koalas **SLEEP** or **REST** for about 18 hours each day.

After a long day of eating and climbing, the little koala is ready to sleep. It curls up on a tree branch for a nap.

Can you find another animal in this book that has a pouch? HINT: Look on page 34.

MOUNTAIN GORILLA

Gorillas live in groups called troops.

A troop may have 30 gorillas. The biggest male is the leader of the family group. Called a silverback, he has silver fur on his back.

There are often other male gorillas in the troop. Females and babies make up the rest of the family.

FACTS

KIND OF ANIMAL
mammal

HOME
two areas in central
Africa

SIZE
male: about as tall as a
tall man; female: about
as tall as a short woman

FOOD
leaves, roots, shoots,
fruits, wild celery, tree
bark and pulp; some-
times insects

SOUNDS
roar, grunt, bark, and
hoot

BABIES
one at a time

Gorillas are usually calm, gentle creatures.

Mothers take care of their babies for several years. Newborns cling to Mom's chest. When babies are about four months old, they ride piggyback.

Gorillas make **NESTS** to sleep in at night. Small gorillas make their nests in the **TREES.** Bigger gorillas make their nests on the ground.

A gorilla's **ARMS** are longer than its body. Imagine being able to **STAND UP** almost straight and touch the ground like a gorilla!

Young gorillas play a lot like you do. They like to chase each other. They climb trees and swing from branches. They pounce on each other and wrestle.

Sometimes they try to get Mom or Dad to play too!

What games do you play with your parents?

FACTS

KIND OF ANIMAL
mammal

HOME
most of North America,
parts of South America,
Europe, and Asia

SIZE
weighs about the same
as a medium-size dog

FOOD
wide variety, including
small animals, plants,
fruits, and nuts

SOUNDS
chitter, whistle, growl,
scream

BABIES
two to six at a time;
usually four

RACCOON

Raccoons are clever rascals.

Raccoon babies practice climbing trees. They can even hang upside down.

Raccoons are usually **MOST ACTIVE** at night.

A raccoon's front paws are almost like your hands. They have fingers.

Raccoons use their fingers to catch food. They eat many things, including fish and frogs.

Raccoons generally live in the **WOODS,** but they also live on farmland, in people's neighborhoods, and even in **BIG CITIES.**

Outside your house you might see a raccoon knock over a garbage can. It is looking for a snack.

Raccoons often live in holes they find in old trees.

NEWBORN raccoons stay inside their den for a few weeks. Then Mom takes them **OUTSIDE**. She teaches them how to hunt for food.

How many raccoons can you spot in this story?

NORTH AMERICAN BEAVER

Beavers build dams.

A beaver family makes its own pond by building a dam.

A **FAMILY** of beavers is called a **COLONY**.

A beaver can **HOLD ITS BREATH** for 15 minutes.

First the beavers use their teeth to chop down trees. They take bites from the trunk until the tree falls over.

FACTS

KIND OF ANIMAL
mammal

HOME
throughout the United
States and Canada

SIZE
weighs about the same
as a big, heavy suitcase

FOOD
water plants, leaves,
grasses, bark, twigs

SOUNDS
whine

BABIES
two to six at a time;
usually four

Then the beavers drag branches and small logs to the spot where they want to make their dam. They pile them up.

The dam slows the stream's flow. The backed-up stream becomes a pond.

The beavers make their home, called a lodge, in the middle of the pond.

The entrance to the beavers' lodge is underwater. Beavers are expert swimmers. They dive and swim to get inside.

A beaver **SLAPS ITS FLAT TAIL** on the surface of the water to warn other beavers of danger.

Inside their lodge, beavers build a floor above the water. The busy beavers can rest at home—safe, warm, and dry.

Can you nibble a big carrot so it looks like the tree on page 96?

TIGER

Tigers are the only striped wild cat.

Tigers hunt by sneaking up on the animals they want to catch.

A tiger's stripes help it stay hidden. Its orange–black–and–white coat blends in with plants and shadows.

FACTS

KIND OF ANIMAL
mammal

HOME
parts of Asia

SIZE
a little longer than
a twin bed

FOOD
several kinds of animals,
especially deer and
wild pigs

SOUNDS
growl, snarl, grunt,
moan, hiss, roar,
and more

BABIES
two to six at a time

The tiger is the **LARGEST** wild cat.

No **TWO TIGERS** have exactly the same **PATTERN** of stripes.

Can you use your finger to trace the whole outline of the tiger hiding at left?

Tigers are good swimmers. They can swim all the way across a river!

Tigers soak in streams or ponds to **COOL OFF.**

Tiger brothers and sisters play. While they wrestle and chase each other, their mother is close by to keep them safe.

Tiger cubs stay with their **MOTHER** until they are about **TWO YEARS** old.

POLAR

The Arctic polar region is in the far north. The Antarctic polar region is in the far south. Both the Arctic and the Antarctic are always cold.

104

HARP SEAL

This seal's coat changes color.

A harp seal can **HOLD ITS BREATH** underwater for 20 minutes. Then it comes to the surface to breathe.

A mother harp seal takes good care of her baby. The baby is called a pup. At first, the pup doesn't look like Mom.

A pup's fluffy white fur helps keep it warm on the ice, where it is born.

A harp seal pup may gain about **80 POUNDS** in 12 days by drinking its **MOTHER'S MILK.**

FACTS

KIND OF ANIMAL
mammal

HOME
North Atlantic and Arctic Oceans

SIZE
weighs about as much as a big professional football player

FOOD
mostly fish

SOUNDS
grunt, bleat

BABIES
one at a time

A newborn harp seal
does not swim. First
it must get bigger
and grow a new coat.

By the time it is two weeks old, the pup is fatter. Its white fur starts to fall out. A silvery coat has grown underneath.

Adult harp seals spend most of their time in the ocean. Their fat keeps them warm while they catch fish and other food to eat.

Out of the water, a harp seal **MOVES** by using its front flippers and **TUMMY** muscles.

Can you move like a seal?

FACTS

KIND OF ANIMAL
bird

HOME
Arctic areas of North America, Europe, and Asia

SIZE
wing tip to wing tip, stretches about as wide as a queen-size bed

FOOD
lemmings, mice, hares, and other small animals

SOUNDS
hoot, click

BABIES
3 to 9 eggs at a time

SNOWY OWL

These birds are hunters.

Snowy owls hunt for food from the air and while on the ground.

The snowy owl is one of the **LARGEST OWLS** in North America. Female snowy owls are larger than males.

Snowy owls see and hear very well. They can spot food as they soar over the ground. They also hunt by standing quietly on the ground as they listen. They are patient hunters.

When they see or hear a small animal moving, they swoop down and grab their dinner with their sharp talons, or claws.

Snowy owls can swallow small **MEALS** whole.

A mother snowy owl lays her eggs on the ground. Her nest is shaped like a shallow bowl in the dirt. Sometimes she lines it with soft feathers and plants.

A snowy owl's entire body is covered in **FEATHERS** that keep it warm. Even its legs and toes have feathers.

After the chicks hatch, their mother stays with them. The dad hunts and brings food to his family.

How long can you stand still like an owl listening for a mouse?

FACTS

KIND OF ANIMAL
mammal

HOME
far north in North America, Europe, and Asia

SIZE
standing on its hind legs, about as tall as the ceiling in a one-story house

FOOD
mostly seals

SOUNDS
growl, hiss, snort, roar

BABIES
usually two

A polar bear has **GIANT FEET** to help it walk on the snow.

POLAR BEAR

This big bear hunts for food on sea ice.

A mother polar bear and her two cubs leave their winter den. It is early spring in the far north.

Polar bears live by the ocean. Their home is usually covered with ice and snow. The polar bears' dense fur coats help keep them warm.

Polar bear **CUBS** stay with their **MOTHER** until they are about two years old.

115

The **POLAR** bear is the **LARGEST** species of bear.

Polar bear cubs love to play. They run and chase each other. They even jump on Mom. Sometimes they climb on top of her!

The mother polar bear is hungry. Her cubs follow along as she looks for food. They learn how to hunt seals by watching her.

Polar bears swim well. They paddle with their front paws. They steer with their back paws. When they climb out of the ocean, they shake the water off their fur.

How do you get dry when you are wet?

117

EMPEROR PENGUIN

These penguins are superdads.

EGG

Emperor penguin mothers and fathers raise their chicks in Antarctica. It is the coldest place on Earth.

After the mother lays an egg, she gives it to the father. He holds it for about two months, keeping it warm.

Penguins are **BIRDS.** But they do not fly. They use their wings to **SWIM.**

POLAR

FACTS

KIND OF ANIMAL
bird

HOME
Antarctica

SIZE
about the height of a
nine-year-old child

FOOD
fish, squid, krill

SOUNDS
cluck, whistle, squawk

BABIES
one at a time

The penguin chick hatches in late winter. Fluffy feathers help keep the little chick warm.

By the end of the summer the young penguins have adult feathers and can swim.

119

There are **18 SPECIES** of penguins, including the emperor penguin shown in the story. Here are just a few species. Which of these is your favorite? Why?

KING

CHINSTRAP

MACARONI

ADÉLIE

GENTOO

ERECT-CRESTED

PARENT TIPS

Extend your child's experience beyond the pages of this book. A visit to the zoo is one great way to continue satisfying your child's curiosity about wildlife. Make a list of the animals in this book and take it with you. At the zoo, have your child check off the animals you see. Here are some other activities you can do with the *National Geographic Little Kids First Big Book of Animals*.

TIME RACES
(EXERCISE)
Cheetahs run fast (p. 8). Challenge your child to run as fast as he can between two specified points while you time him. Then have him travel the same distance running on all fours like a cheetah, hopping like a kangaroo, and squirming like a snake. Compare the times and discuss the concept of fast and slow.

GET DRESSED
(INDEPENDENCE)
Zebras have black-and-white-stripes (p. 12). Have a family zebra day when all of you dress in black-and-white clothing or you all wear stripes.

MEASURE HEIGHT
(MATH)
Giraffes are tall (p. 14). Use a tape measure to determine how high up a wall your child can reach with her hand while standing flat-footed. Compare that height with the height she can reach on her tiptoes.

TAKE A WALK
(EXPLORING)
Garden spiders build webs (p. 18). Go on a spiderweb hunt. Early morning is a great time to spot webs in gardens and meadows because

dew helps make webs more visible. Take along a picnic!

TREASURE HUNT
(COOPERATION)
Lions live in prides, and gray wolves live in packs (pp. 20 and 72). Have two or three of your child's friends over for playtime. Read them the gray wolf and lion pages in the book. Suggest that they cooperate to achieve a goal, just as wolves and lions do. The goal could be figuring out clues to a simple treasure hunt. Give the children a clue to find the next clue. By successfully solving all the clues—using teamwork—they find the "prize." Provide a prize for each of them, or make the prize something that continues cooperation and sharing (for example, cookies to share, a trip together to a playground, art supplies they can all use, or a game they can play together).

SWIM & BREATHE
(WATER SAFETY)
Dolphins breathe air (p. 26). The next time you go swimming, have your child practice getting his face wet. If he is comfortable holding his breath, have him practice blowing bubbles with his face underwater, come up for air—like a dolphin does—and then go back under to blow more bubbles.

TIME CAPSULE
(MEMORY)
Sea turtles bury their eggs in sand (p. 30). Make a time capsule. Have your child collect ten small items—such as a small toy, paper clip, pencil, or stone—and put them into a little waterproof container such as a plastic box to bury and dig up later. Have her dig a hole in the backyard or a sandbox, put the box inside, and cover it. In a day or two ask your child to name everything she can remember putting into the box, as you write it down. Have her dig up the box and compare the list to what she finds in the box.

VISIT AN AQUARIUM
(OBSERVING)
Seahorses are fish (p. 34). At your next opportunity, visit an aquarium with your child. If they have seahorses on exhibit, have your child tell you what animals he thinks seahorses resemble (horse's head, monkey's tail, kangaroo's pouch) and why. As you go through the exhibits, have your child point out the shapes of the different fishes to reinforce the concept of the varieties of fish.

WEATHER CHECK
(MEASURING TEMPERATURE)
Sea otters have thick fur to stay warm (p. 36). Using a weather thermometer, help your child measure the temperature of the inside of your house and compare it to the outside (if different), and to the temperature inside the freezer or refrigerator. Talk about hot and cold temperatures inside versus outside, winter versus summer, etc.

SOCK PUPPET
(CRAFT)
Octopuses have no bones (p. 40).

Make a simple octopus sock doll. Collect a pile of old socks and some newspaper. Roll up a pair of light-colored socks in a ball for the head and mantle. Have your child stuff eight socks with newspaper for the legs. Sew the legs to the head, and then have your child draw eyes and decorate the doll using markers.

SILLY TALK
(HUMOR)
Humpback whales have no teeth (p. 44). Curl your lips over your teeth to show your child how to play a game of "guess what I said" as you each take turns talking "with no teeth."

CONCENTRATION
(MEMORY)
Grunts swim in schools (p. 48). Play concentration with a deck of cards you make with your child. Draw simple fish shapes on 20 index cards. Have your child decorate all the fish in pairs that look alike. (Suggest things such as two fish with pink polka dots, two fish with orange stripes, etc.) Then place the shuffled cards facedown on the floor or a table. Take turns turning over two each. If they match, keep them. If they don't match, turn them back over. When all the cards have been matched, count them to see who has collected the bigger "school" of fish.

COLOR SYMBOLS
(OBSERVATION)
Coral snakes' bright colors send a message (p. 52). Talk with your child about bright colors that send messages in your everyday life. Guide him with examples: a red traffic light or stop sign mean stop; green traffic light means go; and yellow is the color for caution. Ask your child what different colors make him

think of or how different colors make him feel.

JOB FOR PAY
(RESPONSIBILITY)
Meerkats have jobs (p. 54). Ask your child what her "jobs" are. Putting away her toys? Getting dressed? Offer her an opportunity to do a new job to help you and to earn a small amount of money or a special privilege.

SIMON SAYS
(FOLLOWING DIRECTIONS)
Desert jerboas hop like kangaroos (p. 58). Play a game of Simon says with your child and his friends. Make all the directions include ways that animals move—e.g., "Simon says take three gallops like a zebra..., Simon says take two hops forward like a jerboa...." When you do not say "Simon says" (e.g., "Leap like a frog"), the children are supposed to stand still. If they move when they are not supposed to, they're "out."

COLLECT RAIN
(CONSERVATION)
Thorny lizards' spines help them collect water in the desert (p. 60). Talk to your child about the fact that in many places, water is scarce. Suggest that you collect and save rainwater for watering your garden or indoor plants. Set out containers before the next rain. Use the water that you collect the next time you need to water plants.

FROZEN JUICE
(FOLLOWING RECIPE)
Camels' bodies help them stay cool in the hot desert (p. 62). On a hot day, make "juicicles" with your child to help cool off. Freeze juice in ice-cube trays. Insert Popsicle sticks to hold the treats.

MAKE A BOOK
(TELLING A STORY)
Red-eyed tree frogs start out as tadpoles (p. 68). Suggest that your child write a "book" about a little tadpole growing up. Have your child dictate the story as you write. She can illustrate her book by drawing pictures on each page. Have her draw a cover and write a title for her book. A variation on this is to use photographs your child takes.

CLIMB A TREE
(COORDINATION)
Spider monkeys are at home in the trees (p. 76). If you see an appropriately sturdy tree with low branches, help your child climb and play in it. He can hang from a branch and pretend to be a monkey.

ATTRACT WILDLIFE
(PLANTING A GARDEN)
Butterflies start life as caterpillars (p. 80). Help your child plant a butterfly garden in the yard or in a container. Consult your local nursery to find plants that will attract butterflies. Some plants serve as a place for butterflies to lay their eggs; others provide food for the adult butterfly.

20 QUESTIONS
(DEDUCTION)
Koala mothers have pouches (p. 84). Play 20 questions with your child. Take turns with your child hiding objects in your pockets. Have your child hide something first. Ask her "yes" or "no" questions until you can guess what is in her pocket.

FOLLOW THE LEADER
(EXERCISE)
Gorillas live in troops and are led by an adult male (p. 88). Play follow the leader as a family. Take turns being the leader.

MAKE UP JOKES
(HUMOR)
Raccoons are mischievous and clever (p. 92). Sometimes their antics make people laugh. Teach your child some knock-knock jokes or riddles, then invite him to make up jokes of his own.

CREATE A DIORAMA
(CRAFT)
Beavers build dams (p. 96). Help your child build a diorama of a beaver family and its dam. Use clay for the animals, stems with leaves for trees, and twigs and clay for the dam and lodge. Use blue construction paper to represent a stream and pond.

DRAW TIGER MASK
(ART)
Tigers are the only striped wild cat (p. 100). Make tiger masks using paper plates and yarn. Help your child cut out two holes for eyes, and then she can draw the ears, nose, mouth, and whiskers. She can color orange-black-and-white stripes on her tiger's face. Punch two holes on the sides and knot two pieces of yarn through the holes. Now the mask is ready to tie into place.

RHYME WORDS
(LANGUAGE)
Harp seals change their coats (p. 106). Encourage your child to make up a poem or a series of rhyming sentences about seals. Start your child off by asking him what rhymes with "seal" (meal, feel, steal, real, peel, etc.) Then suggest that he make up two funny sentences that rhyme. (Give an example, e.g., "My harp *seal* made me a *meal.*" or "Where did you put the *peel*, you silly *seal*?")

CLUE GAME
(FOLLOWING DIRECTIONS)
Snowy owls hunt (p. 110). Play the "hot and cold" game so that your child can pretend to hunt. Hide a small object while your child closes her eyes. Once the object is hidden, your child begins to look for it. You say "cold" (far away), "warm" (getting closer), or "hot" (about to find it).

VISIT ONLINE
(TECHNOLOGY)
Polar bears find their food in the ocean (p. 114). Go online to watch a polar bear video with your child and learn more about these animals. kids.nationalgeographic.com/Animals/CreatureFeature/Polar-bear

You can also explore the site for more information, videos, and photographs of several other animals in this book.

BOP A BALLOON
(MOTOR SKILLS)
Emperor penguins are superdads (p. 118). After an emperor penguin mother lays her egg, she passes it to the father. The egg cannot touch the ice. See how many times you and your child can hit a balloon back and forth before it touches the ground.

ANIMAL MAP

You can find the areas where the animals in this book live on this map of the world.

ARCTI

NORTH
AMERICA

ATLANTIC
OCEAN

PACIFIC
OCEAN

SOUTH
AMERICA

ATLANTIC
OCEAN

NORTH AMERICA

Arizona coral snake
black-and-yellow
  garden spider
black-handed spider
  monkey
blue morpho
  butterfly
gray wolf
North American
  beaver
polar bear
raccoon
red-eyed tree frog
snowy owl

OCEAN

blue-striped grunt
bottlenose dolphin
giant Pacific octopus
green sea turtle
harp seal
humpback whale
sea otter
short-head seahorse

SOUTH AMERICA

black-handed spider
  monkey
blue morpho
  butterfly
raccoon
red-eyed tree frog

ANTARCTICA

emperor penguin

EUROPE
gray wolf
polar bear
raccoon
snowy owl

ASIA
Bactrian camel
cheetah
desert jerboa
dromedary camel
gray wolf
lion
polar bear
raccoon
snowy owl
tiger

AUSTRALIA
koala
thorny lizard

AFRICA
cheetah
desert jerboa
dromedary camel
giraffe
lion
meerkat
mountain gorilla
zebra

CEAN

EUROPE

ASIA

PACIFIC
OCEAN

AFRICA

INDIAN
OCEAN

AUSTRALIA

ANTARCTICA

GLOSSARY

ALGAE a group of plants and plantlike organisms that usually grow in water

AMPHIBIANS a group of cold-blooded animals with backbones (vertebrate); in some species larval young live in water and breathe through gills; includes frogs, toads, and salamanders

ARACHNIDS a group of animals with no backbone (invertebrate), two body segments, and two to four pairs of legs; includes spiders, scorpions, mites, and ticks

BALEEN a stiff fingernail-like substance that hangs from the upper jaw of baleen whales

BIRDS a group of warm-blooded, vertebrate animals that have feathers, wings, and lay eggs; most can fly

BLOWHOLE the nostril of a cetacean (whales and dolphins), located at the top of its head, through which it breathes

DAM a barrier in a river or stream that slows the flow of water; beavers make dams using logs, mud, and vegetation

DESERT a dry area of land that receives ten inches or less of rain each year

EUCALYPTUS a group of evergreen trees and shrubs native to Australia

FISH a cold-blooded, vertebrate animal that lives in water and breathes through gills

FOREST an area of land covered with trees

GAZELLE any of several species of small- to medium-size antelopes, a group of hoofed mammals

GRASSLAND an area of land where the main plants growing are grasses

HINDI a language of northern India

IMPALA a species of medium-size antelope that is native to southeastern Africa

INSECTS any of a group of small, invertebrate animals with three body segments, one pair of antennae, and three pairs of legs; often have wings

MAMMALS a group of vertebrate animals, including humans, that are warm-blooded, breathe air, have hair, and nurse their young

MOLLUSKS a group of invertebrate animals; usually have a soft body protected by a shell; includes snails and clams

POLAR relating to the regions around the North or South Pole

PREDATOR an animal that eats other animals

PREHENSILE TAIL a tail able to grasp things such as fruit or tree branches

REPTILES a group of vertebrate animals that are cold-blooded, usually slither (such as a snake) or walk on short legs (such as turtles and lizards); generally covered with scales or bony plates

SPECIES a category, or kind, of animal or plant

Prepared by the Book Division

Nancy Laties Feresten, *Vice President, Editor in Chief, Children's Books*

Jonathan Halling, *Design Director, Children's Publishing*

Jennifer Emmett, *Executive Editor, Reference and Solo, Children's Books*

Carl Mehler, *Director of Maps*

R. Gary Colbert, *Production Director*

Jennifer A. Thornton, *Managing Editor*

Staff for This Book

Robin Terry, *Project Editor*

Eva Absher, *Art Direction and Design*

Karine Aigner, Lori Epstein, *Illustrations Editors*

Wanda Jones, Ph.D., *Research*

Grace Hill, *Associate Managing Editor*

Lisa A. Walker, *Production Manager*

Susan Borke, *Legal and Business Affairs*

A special thanks to the staff of
NATIONAL GEOGRAPHIC KIDS magazine
for their contributions to this book.

Manufacturing and Quality Management

Christopher A. Liedel, *Chief Financial Officer*

Phillip L. Schlosser, *Vice President*

Chris Brown, *Technical Director*

Nicole Elliott, *Manufacturing Manager*

Rachel Faulise, *Manufacturing Manager*

COVER, ADAM JONES/ DIGITAL VISION/ GETTY IMAGES; **BACK COVER**, (UP), DIGITAL VISION/ PICTUREREQUEST; (LO), DIGITAL VISION/ GETTY IMAGES; **FRONT MATTER** 1, ALEX COPPEL/ NEWSPIX/ REX USA; 2, STUART WESTMORLAND/ STONE/ GETTY IMAGES; 4, YVA MOMATIUK & JOHN EASTCOTT/ MINDEN PICTURES; **GRASSLAND** 6, INGO ARNDT/ NATUREPL.COM; 8, NOVA STOCK/ IMAGESTATE; 9, ANUP SHAH/ NATUREPL.COM; 10 (LO), ANUP SHAH/ NATUREPL.COM; 10 (UP), C & M DENIS-HUOT/ PETER ARNOLD/ PHOTOSHOT; 11 (LE), ARCO IMAGES/ ALAMY; 11 (RT), ANDY ROUSE/ THE IMAGE BANK/ GETTY IMAGES; 12 (UP), RICHARD DU TOIT/ MINDEN PICTURES; 12 (LO), KARINE AIGNER/ KARINEAIGNER.COM; 13, ANUP SHAH/ NATUREPL.COM; 14, RICHARD DU TOIT/ MINDEN PICTURES; 15, SAMUEL R. MAGLIONE/ PHOTO RESEARCHERS, INC.; 16, ALEX COPPEL/ NEWSPIX/ REX USA; 17, NIGEL J. DENNIS/ PHOTO RESEARCHERS, INC.; 18, STEVE GREER/ ALASKAPHOTOGRAPHICS.COM; 19, JOEL SARTORE/ NATIONAL GEOGRAPHIC IMAGE COLLECTION/ ALAMY; 19, GARY W. CARTER/ ENCYCLOPEDIA/ CORBIS; 20, INGO ARNDT/ MINDEN PICTURES; 21, YVA MOMATIUK & JOHN EASTCOTT/ MINDEN PICTURES; 22, INGO ARNDT/ MINDEN PICTURES; 23 (UP), MITSUYOSHI TATEMATSU/ MINDEN PICTURES; 23 (LO), SUZI ESZTERHAS/ MINDEN PICTURES; **MARINE** 24, MARK CONLIN/ LARRY ULRICH STOCK; 26, STUART WESTMORLAND/ STONE/ GETTY IMAGES; 27, KONRAD WOTHE/ MINDEN PICTURES; 28, O. ALAMANY & E. VICENS/ CORBIS; 29 (LE), KONRAD WOTHE/ MINDEN PICTURES; 29 (RT), DOUG PERRINE/ SEAPICS.COM; 30, MITSUAKI IWAGO/ MINDEN PICTURES; 31 (A), MITSUAKI IWAGO/ MINDEN PICTURES; 31 (B), M. WATSON/ ARDEA; 31 (C), YUSUKE YOSHINO/ MINDEN PICTURES; 31 (D), REINHARD DIRSCHERL/ PETER ARNOLD/ PHOTOSHOT; 32, DOUG PERRINE/ SEAPICS.COM; 32, IMAGE QUEST MARINE; 33 (UP LE), DOUG PERRINE/ SEAPICS.COM; 33 (UP RT), JAMES D. WATT/ SEAPICS.COM; 33 (LO LE), LUIZ CLAUDIO MARIGO/ NATUREPL.COM; 33 (LO RT), IMAGE QUEST MARINE; 34, RUDIE KUITER/ SEAPICS.COM; 35 (UP), RUDIE KUITER/ OCEANWIDEIMAGES.COM; 35 (LO), RUDIE KUITER/ OCEANWIDEIMAGES.COM; 36, SUZI ESZTERHAS/ MINDEN PICTURES; 37, KEVIN SCHAFER/ ZEFA/ CORBIS; 38 (LO), DOC WHITE/ NATUREPL.COM; 38 (UP), SEAPICS.COM; 39 (LO), NORBERT WU/ MINDEN PICTURES; 39 (UP), JOEL W. ROGERS/CORBIS; 40, BRANDON COLE; 41, BRANDON COLE; 42, BRANDON COLE; 43 (UP), BRANDON COLE; 43 (LO), BRANDON COLE; 44, IMAGE QUEST MARINE; 45, BRANDON COLE; 46 (UP), IMAGE QUEST MARINE; 47, BRANDON COLE; 48, WORLDFOTO/ ALAMY; 49 (UP), STEPHEN FRINK COLLECTION/ ALAMY; 49 (LO), DAVID FLEETHAM/ ALAMY; **DESERT** 50, SOLVIN ZANKL/ NPL/ MINDEN PICTURES; 52, RANDALL D. BABB; 53 (RT), JAMES GERHOLDT/ PETER ARNOLD/ PHOTOSHOT; 53 (LE), MICHAEL & PATRICIA FOGDEN/ MINDEN PICTURES; 54, SIMON KING/ NATUREPL.COM; 55, RICHARD DU TOIT/ NATUREPL.COM; 56 (UP), VINCENT GRAFHORST/ FOTO NATURA/ MINDEN PICTURES; 56 (LO), THOMAS DRESSLER/ PHOTOLIBRARY; 57 (LE), SIMON KING/ NATUREPL.COM; 57 (RT), DAVID MACDONALD/ OSF/ PHOTOLIBRARY; 58, WILDLIFE/ PETER ARNOLD/ PHOTOSHOT; 59 (UP), ALAIN DRAGESCO-JOFFE/ BIOSPHOTO; 59 (LO), DANIEL HEUCLIN/ NHPA/ PHOTOSHOT; 60, A.N.T. PHOTO LIBRARY/ NHPA/ PHOTOSHOT; 61, MICHAEL & PATRICIA FOGDEN/ MINDEN PICTURES; 62, BRUNO MORANDI/ HEMIS/ CORBIS; 63, HANNE & JENS ERIKSEN/ NATUREPL.COM; 64, A.N.T. PHOTO LIBRARY/ PHOTO RESEARCHERS, INC.; 65, REUTERS/ LANDOV; **FOREST** 66, KLEIN-HUBERT/ KIMBALL STOCK; 68, TIM FLACH/ STONE/ GETTY IMAGES; 69 (RT), MICHAEL DURHAM/ MINDEN PICTURES; 69 (LE), MICHAEL & PATRICIA FOGDEN MINDEN PICTURES; 70 (LO), GAIL SHUMWAY/ TAXI/ GETTY IMAGES; 70 (UP), MICHAEL & PATRICIA FOGDEN/ MINDEN PICTURES; 71, GAIL SHUMWAY/ TAXI/ GETTY IMAGES; 72, MARY CLAY/ ARDEA; 73, LISA HUSAR/ TEAM HUSAR; 74, CHRISTINA KRUTZ/ AGE FOTOSTOCK/ PHOTOLIBRARY; 75 (UP), LISA HUSAR/ TEAM HUSAR; 75 (LO), LISA HUSAR/ TEAM HUSAR; 76, MICHAEL TURCO; 77, THOMAS MARENT/ MINDEN PICTURES; 78, ART WOLFE; 79, THOMAS MARENT/ ARDEA; 80, BASCO/ GT PHOTO; 80, BASCO/ GT PHOTO; 81, WILLIAM T. HARK; 82 (LO), MICHAEL & PATRICIA FOGDEN/ MINDEN PICTURES; 82 (UP), THOMAS MARENT/ MINDEN PICTURES; 83 (UP LE), CHRIS MARTIN BAHR/ ARDEA; 83 (UP RT), THOMAS MARENT/ MINDEN PICTURES; 83 (LO LE), KIM TAYLOR/ NATUREPL.COM ; 83 (LO RT), JURGEN & CHRISTINE SOHNS/ FLPA/ MINDEN PICTURES; 84, HANS & JUDY BESTE/ ARDEA; 85, KLEIN/ PETER ARNOLD/ PHOTOSHOT; 86 (LO), MITSUAKI IWAGO/ MINDEN PICTURES; 86 (UP), POWERHOUSE DIGITAL PHOTOGRAPHY LTD/ ALAMY; 87 (RT), FRANS LANTING/ MINDEN PICTURES; 87 (LE), DANITA DELIMONT/ ALAMY; 88, ANDY ROUSE/ NATUREPL.COM; 89, INGO ARNDT/ NATUREPL.COM; 90 (UP), SUZI ESZTERHAS/ MINDEN PICTURES; 90 (LO), GERRY ELLIS/ MINDEN PICTURES; 91 (UP), PAUL HOBSON/ NATUREPL.COM; 91 (LO), ANDY ROUSE/ NATUREPL.COM; 92, LISA HUSAR/ TEAM HUSAR; 93, LISA HUSAR/ TEAM HUSAR; 94 (UP), PETER WEIMANN/ PHOTOLIBRARY; 94 (LO), MICHAEL DURHAM/ MINDEN PICTURES; 95, AGE FOTOSTOCK/ SUPERSTOCK; 96, DOMINIQUE BRAUD/ AMAZING ANIMALS; 97, ERWIN & PEGGY BAUER/ PHOTOSHOT; 98 (UP), YVA MOMATIUK & JOHN EASTCOTT/ MINDEN PICTURES; 98 (LO), LARRY LEE PHOTOGRAPHY/ SURF/ CORBIS; 99 (UP), TOM & PAT LEESON; 99 (LO), ERWIN & PEGGY BAUER/ WILDSTOCK; 100, MICHAEL NICHOLS/ NATIONALGEOGRAPHICSTOCK.COM; 101, RENEE LYNN/ CORBIS; 102 (LO), DLILLC/ CORBIS; 102 (UP), FRANCOIS SAVIGNY/ ANIMALS ANIMALS; 103, RENEE LYNN/ CORBIS; **POLAR** 104, JOHNNY JOHNSON/ ALASKASTOCK.COM; 106, MICHIO HOSHINO/ MINDEN PICTURES; 107, MICHIO HOSHINO/ MINDEN PICTURES; 108, MICHIO HOSHINO/ MINDEN PICTURES; 109 (UP), DOUG ALLAN/ NATUREPL.COM; 109 (LO), WOODFALL/ PHOTOSHOT; 110, SCOTT LINSTEAD/ VIREO; 111, SCOTT LINSTEAD/ FOTO NATURA/ MINDEN PICTURES; 112 (UP), SCOTT LINSTEAD/ FOTO NATURA/ MINDEN PICTURES; 112 (LO), JIM ZIPP/ ARDEA; 113, (UP), WINFRIED WISNIEWSKI/ FOTO NATURA/ MINDEN PICTURES; 113 (LO), DANIEL J. COX/ NATURALEXPOSURES.COM; 114, MITSUAKI IWAGO/ MINDEN PICTURES; 115, MATTHIAS BREITER/ MINDEN PICTURES; 116, MIKE & LISA HUSAR/ TEAM HUSAR; 117 (UP), JOHNNY JOHNSON/ ANIMALS ANIMALS; 117 (LO), STEVEN KAZLOWSKI/ ALASKASTOCK.COM; 118, FRANS LANTING/ MINDEN PICTURES; 119 (RT), KONRAD WOTHE/ MINDEN PICTURES; 119 (LE), MARTHA HOLMES/ NPL/ MINDEN PICTURES; 120 (UP), ARCO IMAGES GMBH/ ALAMY; 120 (LO), JAN VERMEER/ FOTO NATURA/ MINDEN PICTURES; 121 (UP LE), THEO ALLOFS/ MINDEN PICTURES; 121 (UP RT), YVA MOMATIUK & JOHN EASTCOTT/ MINDEN PICTURES; 121 (LO LE), YVA MOMATIUK & JOHN EASTCOTT/ MINDEN PICTURES; 121 (LO RT), TUI DE ROY/ MINDEN PICTURES; **BACK MATTER** 126, IMAGE99/ JUPITERIMAGES;128, SUZI ESZTERHAS/ MINDEN PICTURES.